Pierre Blot

Prof. Blot's Cookery

Pierre Blot

Prof. Blot's Cookery

ISBN/EAN: 9783744785143

Printed in Europe, USA, Canada, Australia, Japan

Cover: Foto ©Lupo / pixelio.de

More available books at **www.hansebooks.com**

"...st honored of Professors is Professor Blot."

ROF. BLOT'S

R. Y.

LORIN

BROTH, SOUPS, &c.

1.—BROTH.

The following is a stock for soups and gravies:

Put three pounds of lean beef—any part of the animal—in about three quarts of cold water, salt and place it over a lively fire. When at a boiling point take off with a skimmer the scum on the surface; afterward add a small quantity of cold water together with half a middling sized carrot, cut into small pieces; a small piece of turnip—half as much as of carrot; one leek; an onion with two cloves stuck in it; a stalk of celery cut into several pieces, and a bay leaf. Care must be taken in allowing the broth to boil gently, and for the space of five hours. Good broth is as clear as spring water; milky-colored broth is the result of allowing it to boil too much. When the broth has boiled for the time indicated, the onion, clove and celery are to be taken out and cast aside, and the whole strained before serving. Burnt sugar is sometimes used in giving the liquid color.

For inferior broth take a pound of any kind of bones, two quarts of cold water, a small carrot, small turnip, one leek, one onion with two cloves stuck in it, a piece of celery, salt, &c. Simmer six to eight hours, skimming carefully at intervals. Strain carefully and keep for use.

In summer you should not attempt to keep broth over two days, as it will sour.

2.—POTAGE JULIENNE.

The Julienne Soup, the making of which is given below, becomes Potage à la Colbert when one forced egg is added for every person. To make it Potage Printanier, to carrots and turnips given below must be added asparagus tops, half a dozen small radishes, two tablespoonfuls of green peas. To make it Potage au Riz take two tablespoonfuls of rice, boil gently till tender in a pint of water, drain through a culander, and put the rice into the Julienne ten minutes before taking off the fire.

To make the Julienne for eight persons take two carrots and two turnips, cut them into thin slices, put into a saucepan, with one tablespoonful of butter, and fry. When it is stewed, a small leek cut up and put in and stirred again. Add nearly a quart of broth, and simmer gently till the vegetables are done.

3.—SOUP CONSOMMÉ.

Take three quarts of broth, strain it through a sieve or a strainer (not a culander). Put one, two, three or four chickens in whole, and simmer two and a half hours. Take out the chickens, and your potage is done. The pot must be skimmed in simmering. You need not have very young chickens or fat ones.

4.—POTAGE AU CHASSEUR

May be made with game or rabbits. When these are scarce you can use a pigeon.

When you use rabbit take head, neck, heart, &c., and if you have cold fowl bones break them up and throw them in.

If you use pigeon, the end of the legs and wing are cut off, then the skin on the back of the neck, take out the crop and clean it. Cut the pigeon open a little on the side to clean it, just under the leg. When you cook birds whole always clean them so. Brown the pieces, liver, breast, &c., in a pan with butter. Add broth, and let it boil.

Simmer an hour and a half, skimming off the fat. Take it off and turn it through a strainer.

5.—MOCK TURTLE SOUP.

One table spoon of butter in a saucepan on the fire,

add one table spoon of flour, stir, and when it browns add one quart of broth and one onion, with two cloves stuck in it. After simmering ten or fifteen minutes, put in one gill of wine, according to taste, or three gills.

When it is done, turn it in a soup dish. In the dish half of a lemon cut in small slices, and one egg boiled hard and cut in small slices. Some use more eggs. Just before serving add a gill of rum or brandy. Cut into it some dice of calfs' head boiled.

6.—POTAGE AUX NOUILLES.

Put half a pound of flour on the board, mix it with an egg, salt, a teaspoonfull of chopped parsley. It makes a thick, dry paste. Roll it with a pin, sprinkling flour to keep it from sticking, till it is thick as possible. Roll it flat, and hang it over a chair back to dry. When it has dried half an hour, cut the paste in small narrow strips like a pencil.

Put a pot of broth on the fire. When it boils drop in the nouilles strips.

7.—POTAGE VELOUTÉ.

Three yolks of eggs in a soup dish, stirred up. Turn in a quart of hot broth, stirring fast. You may use more eggs, if you like.

8.—POTAGE TAPIOCA.

Put four tablespoons of tapioca in a saucepan, with three pints of warm broth. Simmer, stirring occasionally.

You may prepare a soup in exactly the same way with corn-starch, or arrow-root, or fecula, or sago, or semoulina.

Burnt sugar is sometimes used to color broth or gravy.

9.—POTAGE AU RIZ.

Soak your rice in cold water to wash it. Put four ounces of rice and half a pint of cold water on the fire. At the first boiling add a little more than a pint of milk, and keep it on the fire.

As it cooks add another pint of milk, gradually, as needed. Barley or vermicelli may be prepared the same.

10.—POTAGE PURÉE.

Use either one or more of asparagus, carrots, cauli-flowers, celery, cucumbers peeled and seeded, beets, lettuce, parsnips, turnips, squash, sorrel, tomato, Jerusalem artichoke, or other vegetable. Cauli-flowers are blanched in hot water, with a little flour to keep them white. The other things in hot water only. They are cut in small pieces when used.

When made with peas it is called potage purée à la chantilly,—with carrots, à la crecy,—with red beans, à la conde.

You may make a purée with water and butter, but broth is better.

Take peas, shell a proper quantity, simmer in a quart of broth till done. Break into the soup some pieces of bread, browned, when you serve.

11.—POTAGE JULIENNE MAIGRE.

Carrot and turnips in thin fillips, asparagus tops in small pieces, and green peas.

Put a tablespoon of butter in a saucepan on the fire. When melted add the vegetables, and stir a little. When partly fried add a quart of water, and then put in the peas and asparagus. As the water boils away add a little more warm water. Salt and pepper to taste.

12.—TOMATO SOUP.

Throw them in boiling water for a minute; skin them; mash them through a strainer or seive so as to clear skins or seeds, and finish with boiling in broth, like a purée potage.

13.—POTAGE AU FROMAGE.

When maccaroni is cooked tender, turn it into broth, on the fire.

Put cheese grated in the soup dish, and turn the

macaroni soup over it. Vermicelli may be used the same way.

14.—TURTLE SOUP.

You must have the turtle alive. Cut the head off and let it bleed to death. Boil the turtle till the shells can be separated, and the meat is cooked. Take off the gall bladder, and if you find a black ball (if there is any) throw it away.

Put butter and flour in a saucepan, and the pieces of turtle, and cook a little. Pour in some broth.

Put in your dish a lemon cut in slices, an egg boiled and cut up. Pour over it the soup and meat, and serve.

FISH.

15.—BAKED FISH.

After washing, a shad is wiped dry, inside and outside, next buttered, salted and peppered, with bread crumbs, a little chopped parsnip and the juice of half a lemon squeezed on the outside; then place in a bake-pan and put in the oven.

Halibut, haddock, cod, or other fish, do the same way. Eat with cream of flour, butter, &c.

16.—BOILED FISH.

Take a fish of dark flesh. Put in a pan and just cover with cold water, two or three slices of carrot, the same of onion, two stalks of parsley and thyme, a clove of garlic. After it arrives at the boiling point boil only two minutes.

17.—SAUCE GENEVOISE.

Fry a piece of onion chopped fine in half a tablespoonful of butter. When browned add a teaspoonful of flour and brown it. Add a gill of the water the fish was boiled in, a half a gill of white wine or a teaspoonful of vinegar, shred in some mushrooms, and cook a little while.

18.—SMELTS.

Have a frying pan full of hot fat on the fire. Put a skewer through them at the gills, and lay them in the pan, half a dozen on the skewer, the ends of the skewer resting on the edge of the pan.

19.—FISH, CAPER SAUCE.

Take a bass. Pour boiling water over it, and in a few moments the scales will scrape off easily. Put the bass on the fire, just covered with cold water, with a little pepper and salt, slice of onion and carrot, and one clove of garlic.

A little butter and flour on the fire. When melted, add half a pint of the fish water and stir, with a little touch of vinegar. Throw in your capers just as you are ready to turn it over the fish.

20.—CODFISH, WITH EGG SAUCE.

Chop two or three hard boiled eggs fine. Put a lump of butter as large as an egg in a saucepan on the fire. When melted add a little lemon juice, and the chopped egg, and after stirring a little turn it over the fish.

Always put a fish in cold water; when it boils, let a two-pound fish cook two or three minutes, a six-pound fish six or eight minutes.

21.—BAKED FISH.

Put fish in a bakepan with a little water, a few slices of onion and carrot, which add their sugar to the sauce. No good gravy can be made without these two vegetables. Parsley, thyme and bay leaf (see veal). If the fish water dries too fast while baking, add a little warm water. A fork will tell when the fish is done by its flaking. Take out the fish and simmer the pan on the fire to make gravy. A little broth is an addition.

22.—FISH A LA BECHAMEL.

Take cold water, salt, and the thyme and parsley seasoning, and put your halibut in just covered. When it boils, let it boil but two minutes.

Take a tablespoon of butter and one of flour, and mix well on the fire. Add a pint of the fish water. A few drops of lemon juice will give a pique to the sauce bechamel. The fish will be dished, and the sauce poured over it.

23.—FISH STUFFED.

Take bread and soak it in milk, and then squeeze it out. Mix in an egg and a little parsley and seasoning.

Take your fish and draw it from a cut just under the head so as not to cut the stomach. Put the bread into the fish and put the fish on a bakepan with a little butter under and on top. Salt and pepper. Put a little broth to cover the bottom of the pan, and set it in the oven.

Fish to bake requires fifteen to twenty minutes. Then put a little lemon juice in the gravy.

24.—FISH A LA MAITRE D'HOTEL.

Take a fresh mackerel (or other fish). Split it down the back, and put it in a pan in the oven without anything with it or on it, and cook it. When fish comes off the bones easy with a fork it is done.

For sauce a small tablespoon of butter and a teaspoon and a half of chopped parsley in a saucepan on the fire; the juice of half a lemon.

25.—FISH, ANCHOVY SAUCE.

Put two pounds black-flesh fish on the fire, just covered with cold water, slices of onion and carrot, parsley, thyme and a bay leaf, salt and pepper. After it begins to boil keep it on two minutes.

Put half a tablespoon of butter and flour in a pan; when melted, stir in a gill of the fish water; then a tablespoon of essence of anchovy.

26.—FISH, MAYONNAISE SAUCE.

If you have cold fish left over from a previous day's cookery use it.

Put two yolks of eggs in a bowl, and add four or five tablespoons of olive oil as you stir, little by little. It is best to do this in a cool place, or on a window, opened. When it is thick put in one half tablespoonful of vinegar, some salt and pepper. Add mustard if you like.

Spread the cream over the cold fish or over meat of.any kind, and serve.

27.—SOLE NORMANDE.

As there are no soles, use a flounder. Remove the skin and pull off the flesh from the backbone in four long fillets. There will be two large and two small fillets. Butter a flat pan and put in the fillets.

Chop some onion fine and spread over the fish. Then pour in a gill of claret and less of sherry or other light wine. Salt and pepper. Add a gill of broth (soup stock.) Place it in the oven.

28.—COURT BOUILLON.

Take any kind of black fleshed fish. Lay it on a pan on slices of onion and carrot. Half cover it with wine and water. Put the peel of the lemon, salt, pepper and a bunch of seasoning. When done so very little its over.

When done, place it in a dish, and put the pan back on the fire.

29.—SAUCE BOUILLON.

Take the fish water, add a few slices of carrot or turnip, a bunch of parsley, thyme, &c., and when cooked down reasonably pour it over the fish.

30.—BISQUE OF LOBSTER.

Always buy lobsters alive, if possible. A lobster is poisonous if boiled after dead. Put the lobster alive in a fish kettle of cold water, and put it on a sharp fire. The lobster drowns before the water gets warm. When it turns red, twenty minutes or more, it is done. Break it in the middle, and drain in a culander. Split the tail part in two and take the black vein out. Take the claws for a salad. Take off the red (coral) meat. Pound the shells and body and legs, &c., and put it in a pot of water. After cooking ten minutes add a pint of broth, and simmer ten minutes more. Add either water or broth, and simmer longer.

Strain the liquor through a culander, and put the liquor back on the fire, with a few toasts of bread, and simmer it. Press it and the bread through a culander. Mix the coral and the greyish part of the lobster with butter, and put it in the soup dish.

A bisque may also be made with crabs, and further South with crawfish.

31.—LOBSTER FARCI (STUFFED.)

Take off the shells of a boiled lobster carefully.

Chop a piece of onion and fry it with a little butter. When it is partly fried, add a teaspoon of flour. Chop your lobster fine and put that in the pan, and stir so as partly to fry. Add half a pint of milk and stir again. Stir it frequently to keep it from burning. Add pepper and salt. Lay the pieces of the body shell in a pan, and fill them with the mixture. Also the large claws. Bake them in an oven.

32.—OYSTERS A LA POULETTE.

One pint of oysters, and juice, on the fire, in a saucepan. Skim as the scum rises.

Take another pan. Mix a tablespoonful of butter and one of flour, on the fire; when melted, stir in half a pint of milk.

When the oysters boil up, put in the milk, and salt to taste, and serve.

Clean some large oyster shells, and serve the poulette in them; when so served it is called huitres en coquilles.

33.—MATELOTE.

Take any kind of black flesh fish. Take eels and

bass for instance. Cut them in small pieces about two inches long. Put a lump of fat in a saucepan. When melted put in the fish. Add a bunch of seasoning composed of parsley, thyme and garlic.

To make it really excellent make it three or four days before eating, and warm it every day by setting the pan in boiling water.

Put a small tablespoonful of flour into the pot, gill of claret wine, and a little over a gill of broth, for a pound of fish. Also an onion.

MEATS.

34.—BREAKFAST STEAK.

The fire must be quick, and three minutes is sufficient for both sides.

For two pounds of steak half a tablespoonful of butter is sufficient. The steaks are salted and peppered before being put into the pan. Sprinkle water cress with salt, pepper and vinegar, and dress around the steak after it is dished.

This is not frying. To fry is to immerse in fat. Doughnuts are fried.

35.—BAKED BEEF.

The mode of baking beef was very similar to that usually practiced here, with salt, pepper and butter, and an oven not too quick. When sauce piquante is used with it, the same should be mixed with the beef gravy.

36.—SAUCE PIQUANTE.

Fry a piece of onion chopped fine in a half tablespoonful of butter. When brown add a teaspoonful of flour and brown that. Then add two tablespoons each of vinegar and broth. Heat in it some small slices of cold meat. Add a little chopped parsley before using.

37.—FILLET OF BEEF.

This piece was from the round, three and a half pounds. It was a flat piece, and the top was stuck thickly with little pegs of new salt pork, put into little slits made in the beef. This is called larding. Put it in a pan. A little butter on the beef, salt and pepper. A little broth, just to cover the bottom of the pan. Put the pan in the oven.

When you bake meat, the oven is generally warmest on the top. You can grease a paper and lay on top of the meat. It prevents the steam from rising, and keeps the top of the meat or bird moist. You need only to baste the paper occasionally, not the meat, to keep it from burning. Some meats require less time than others. Pork and veal, to be healthy, should always be overdone.

38.—SAUCE FOR THE BEEF.

Put in a small saucepan a table spoon of butter and melt it. Add one spoonful of flour. When turning brown add a little over half a pint of broth. Stir. Afterwards not quite a gill of white wine. Two teaspoons of vinegar may be used instead of wine, but it is inferior. (This was Sauterne). Put in a little bunch of seasoning (see veal), three or four mushrooms, &c.

39.—BOILED BEEF IN MIROTON.

You may take the beef you have boiled for broth. A remnant of roast or baked beef will do as well.

Slice two large onions for each pound of beef. Put the onions in a saucepan with a teaspoonful of butter, a little salt and pepper. When turning brown, add a little broth, to simmer.

Cut the beef in small slips or slices. When the onions are nearly cooked, salt and pepper, and add the beef. After some cooking put in a teaspoonful . of vinegar.

40.—BEEF BOILED, HOLLANDAISE SAUCE.

Take a pound or more of beef, as in miroton (see above) and cut it in fillets (slips like a half a pencil).

Put a small tablespoonful of fat in a saucepan, and when melted put the fillets of beef in. Stir so as to fry the pieces. Then just cover the beef with broth. After cooking stir a little lemon juice and a teaspoonful of chopped parsley, boil up once and it is done.

For sauce stir one yolk of egg with a little lemon juice and turn in.

41.—BEEF AU GRATIN.

Take cold beef, either boiled or roasted, and cut it in thin slices. Grease a tin pan with butter, dust with bread crumbs, put in a little chopped parsley, and lay on the slices of beef. Put salt and pepper and parsley on top, dust with bread crumbs, drop on lemon juice, a little broth just to cover the bottom of the pan, and place it in the oven.

42.—BEEF A LA MODE.

Take a piece of thick meat, two or two and a half inches thick. Run slips of salt pork through from side to side, by cutting slits.

Put a teaspoon of butter in a saucepan. Melt. Put in the beef. When fried a few minutes turn it over. When browned on both sides add one gill of broth. Then set where it will only simmer, or boil lightly.

After a while add a half pint more broth, salt and butter, a bunch of seasoning (parsley, bay leaf, and one clove of garlic,) one onion whole, with three cloves stuck in it. Simmer on both sides, for some time.

43.—STUFFED SHOULDER OF VEAL.

Cut in straight and take out the bones, which will do for soup next day. For stuffing take one pound of sausage meat, chopped and mixed with two ounces of bread, the bread to be soaked in water and squeezed dry with the hand; one teaspoonful of chopped parsley, salt and pepper as best suits the taste, one egg, a clove of garlic, chopped fine; mix with a wooden spoon. Some persons prefer to use onions in stuffing. . Put the stuffing into the bone hole and sew up.

The meat thus prepared, with the first bone remaining in it, spread over with a small quantity of butter, with a sprinkling of salt and pepper. The pan must contain just broth enough to keep the meat wet at the bottom. During the process of baking more broth is added to supply the place of that which evaporates.

44.—VEAL IN BLANQUETTE.

Cut veal in small pieces. Say from the neck and breast, three pounds. Soak in cold water, fifteen to thirty minutes. Put it in a saucepan, and cover it with cold water. Boil. Skim the scum. Add two whole onions with a clove to each; then two stalks of parsley, one of thyme, and a small bay leaf, tied together in a little bunch; add salt.

Mix well in a bowl a teaspoon of butter, one of flour. Take a little of the veal water, and mix in so as to melt the butter and mix the flour. Then turn it into the saucepan and simmer.

Just before serving, a few drops of lemon juice may be added. Also a yolk of egg mixed in a bowl with some of the gravy. Your dish is then ready.

45.—VEAL IN GALANTINE.

Take a piece of veal, say three pounds, the leaner the better. Cut it in small slices, and rather thin.

The spices used are, four or five stalks of parsley and a little piece of onion, chopped fine.

Put a layer of slices of pork, thin as possible, on the bottom of a pan. Then a layer of veal, then the chopped parsley and onion, and a little salt and pepper. Another layer of salt pork, one of sausage meat, (and, if you like it, one of ham).

Another layer of veal and parsley. Then another

of salt pork. Thus far, to fill the mould we have used two and a half pounds of veal, one of sausage meat, and one half pound of pork. Add a wine glass of brandy and a little broth. Then place in a moderate oven.

This dish may be eaten cold for breakfast.

46.—VEAL IN RAGOUT.

Take the bony ends of chops or piece of the neck, cut in small pieces, and put them in a pan on the fire with a little butter, and stir so as to brown. Afterward add a little flour and stir. Add a half pint of broth and stir again. Salt and pepper. Two small onions, two cloves, bunch of seasoning. Simmer.

Cut six new potatoes in moderate, walnut-sized pieces, and put them in the pan with the veal.

47.—CHOPS (VEAL) IN PAPILLOTES.

Take the good part of the chop left from the ragout. Cut sheets of white letter paper in heart shape as large as possible. Fry the chop on both sides, till three-quarters done, with salt and pepper. Any kind of small bird can be treated so by splitting, and a prairie hen by being cut in nine pieces. Grease the paper with a little olive oil.

Have a mixture of bread crumbs and chopped parsley, with salt and pepper. Put a little of this on one side of the paper, lay on a chop, cover with the other half of the paper, and double down the edges.

Put the papered chops in a bake pan. Pour over them a gravy made by stirring a little broth in the pan in which they were fried. Put the bake pan in the oven.

The chops are served as they are, in the paper—a chop to each plate.

48.—FRICANDEAU.

This is made always with veal. The piece used here weighed three pounds. It was a thick slice from the upper part of the leg. Take out the round bone. Lard one side of it by sticking in little slits all over it slips of salt pork.

Place in a bakepan an ounce or thereabout of salt pork, and broth enough to cover the pan a fourth of an inch. Lay in the veal. Place the pan in the oven. After some time baste and salt the top.

When the broth is nearly baked out add half a gill more. After half an hour or so baste a second time.

If there is not gravy enough after you dish add a little broth to the pan.

It may be served with "spinach au jus" or with sorrel.

49.—COTELETTES.

Cutlets, or mutton chops. Simmer a few thin slices of carrots and turnips in a little water. Put in butter, when it is melted add the chops. Fry them on both sides a little. Then take out the chops and vegetables. Put in the pan a teaspoonful of flour and stir it. When the flour is turning brown add a gill of broth. Stir it a while, and then put back the chops, carrots and turnips, and cook till done.

50.—LEG OF MUTTON BOILED, CAPER SAUCE.

Wrap the leg up in a towel, over and over, tying up the ends. Put it in boiling water. A leg of mutton or an old turkey are the only fresh meats that are not spoiled by boiling. When done, take off the towel and dish it.

Set a tablespoonful of butter in the pan with the same of flour and stir. In two minutes set it a little aside, so it will not boil. Then put in a teaspoonful or more of capers, and at once turn it over the mutton.

51.—KIDNEY SAUTE.

This is a breakfast dish. Any kidney will do. If you use a pork kidney, it must be cut in half and soaked in warm water.

Take a beef kidney for instance. Cut it in small pieces. Put a little butter in a pan ; add a pinch of chopped onion. When well colored by frying, add the kidney. Afterward stir in half a teaspoonful of flour fast, and half a gill of white wine mixed in a bowl with some of the juice. A teaspoonful of chopped parsley may be added to the simmering mass.

52.—SWEETBREAD.

Soak sweetbread in cold water for about half an hour. Pick out the little veins and skin. Throw in boiling water for three minutes. Then put them under a board for half an hour, with a board on to flatten them. Cut slits in and insert slivers of salt pork over the top.

Put them in a bakepan with a little salt pork, and broth to cover the bottom of the pan. Put them in the oven.

When baked (say an hour or more) add a little broth, and in a few minutes serve.

53.—CALF'S HEAD A LA POULETTE.

Soak it in cold water two or three hours, to get out the blood. Put it in a pan on the fire and cover it with cold water. Salt, pepper, carrot, an onion with two cloves in it, one turnip, two or three stalks of parsley, one of thyme, a bay leaf, and boil it all gently till done, say about two hours.

For sauce a tablespoon of butter and flour, stirred in a pan on the fire, and add a little over a pint of the water in which the head was cooked. Stir. A teaspoon of parsley, chopped, a little lemon juice. If not thick enough, add a little butter and flour which has been mixed in a bowl, and wetted with a little of the hot broth. Cook a little and turn it over the head with a few drops of lemon juice.

54.—SUCKING PIG.

Soak the soft part of the head and squeeze it out with the hand. Mix it in a bowl with two pounds of sausage meat. Chop fine five or six stalks of parsley and a little onion, and mix it in the bowl. Salt and pepper. Two eggs broken in. When well mixed, put it in the pig and sew it up.

(In winter, a good stuffing is boiled chestnuts, with the skins peeled off. Cooked rice makes a good stuffing.)

Put a stone in the pig's mouth to keep it open. After it is baked you send it to the table with a red apple in the mouth. After the head is cut off, the best piece in the animal is the next cut on the neck, and so on.

Before putting it in the oven, put salt and pepper on the top of the beast. The pig must be turned when browned, and three hours will bake well.

Serve it with maitre d'hotel sauce or currant jelly.

55.—MUTTON IN HARICOT.

Take a neck or breast piece cut in chunks. Put a half tablespoon of butter in a pan, and then the mutton. Cook it till it browns. Stir in a table spoon of flour. Put in two onions, some broth, a bunch of parsley and thyme seasoning, a bay leaf, salt and pepper to taste.

Add five raw potatoes, cut in quarters. If the broth has boiled away, add a little more. When the potatoes are cooked the haricot is done.

56.—VENISON A LA REVIGOTE.

Pork may be prepared in the same way, as we have no venison here. Two pounds of pork, half a tablespoon of butter, salt and pepper, in a pan on the fire. When the pork browns a little, turn it over. When browned on both sides put it in the oven. Venison must be underdone and pork overdone.

The revigote sauce. Slice a medium sized onion and set it on the fire with a gill of vinegar. Good cider vinegar is as good as you can get. Pure wine vinegar cannot be had for three times the price they charge for wine vinegar.

In another pan half a tablespoon of butter and flour each, and when it browns add half a pint of broth and stir a little. When the vinegar in the first pan is nearly evaporated, turn them in together, stir, and then strain the whole back into the second pan to separate the onion, and it is done.

57.—VENISON, ROBERT SAUCE.

In the absence of venison, take beef or pork. The professor used a piece of pork. Put the pork in a bakepan, with a little salt. Its own fat will keep it from burning. (Beef and venison will want a little broth in the bottom.) Put it in the oven. After half an hour's cooking turn it over.

The pork must be left in the oven till overdone. Venison must always be underdone. Dish and pour over it the Robert sauce.

58.—ROBERT SAUCE.

One gill of vinegar and two onions on the fire till the vinegar has boiled away. Put a tablespoon of butter and one of flour in another pan and stir; when it browns put in a little broth and stir. Turn it into the pan with the onion, and then the whole back again into the second pan.

59.—BOILED HAM.

Soak the ham in cold water from three to six hours, according to its saltness. Put it in the kettle and entirely cover it with cold water. Put in a bunch of seasoning, an onion and four cloves. A half pint of white wine will improve the taste. Also a little hay. When cooked, let it cool in the water, and take off the end of the bone. Garnish it by sticking cloves in it.

60.—BAKED FRESH PORK.

Take a leg of fresh pork, skin it, put it in a vessel. Take salt, pepper, two tablespoons of vinegar, four tablespoons of sweet oil, four bay leaves, four sage leaves, and a gill of white wine, and with this mixture baste the leg several times a day, for three days or so, and then bake it, well done.

FOWLS, GAME, &c.

61.—CHICKEN FRICASSEE.

A chicken anywhere under a year old will do.

Cut it in small pieces, put them in a saucepan, just cover them with cold water, throw in a pinch of salt, and cook. Any bird, or a rabbit may be used.

For gravy, a small onion with two cloves planted in it; a bunch of seasoning, made of parsley, bayleaf, &c.; salt and pepper to taste; half a spoonful of butter; half spoonful of flour; mix well together and turn in with the chicken. Some of the juice of the chicken may be turned into the bowl containing the butter and flour to avoid having any lumps in the flour. A few drops of lemon juice may be squeezed into the pan, and those who choose may stir in the yolk of an egg.

62.—CHICKEN SAUTE.

Cut a tender young chicken in fourteen or fifteen pieces. Put half a tablespoonful of butter in a saucepan on the fire; when melted, put in the chicken, and stir so as to color or cook the pieces all over. Add half a pint of broth, and not quite a gill of white wine, claret or sauterne. Sherry will do for a substitute for white wine, but less must be used.

After simmering put in a bunch of seasoning, (parsley, thyme, and a bay leaf), and several mushrooms. A little broth added will improve the sauce. Serve warm. Any bird or a rabbit may be used.

63.—PIGEON IN CRAPAUDINE.

Take the pigeon, split it down the back, and cut off the ends of the legs and of the wings. Flatten it out and dry it with a cloth. Mix bread crumbs with a little chopped parsley, salt and pepper. Wet the pigeon lightly with sweet oil, and roll it in the crumbs. Broil it on a gridiron.

For sauce, melt a teaspoonful of butter in a saucepan, put in a tablespoon of flour, and stir till brown. Then a little onion chopped fine, and stir it till fried. Add three tablespoons of vinegar. Afterward, half a teaspoon of chopped parsley, broth, salt and pepper.

64.—CHICKEN BONED.

Any bird is boned in the same way, the larger the better. Take a dry picked chicken. Cut off the legs at the first joint. Split the back skin from the neck to the rump. Break the wing joint, and the wing comes off with the rest. With a small, sharp knife, peel off all the flesh, cutting close to the bone. You get off the flesh and skin in one piece, with the legs and wings on. Then cut out the leg bones and the wing bones.

The chicken weighed 3 1-2 pounds. There was also used 3-4 pounds of ham, 3 sheeps' tongues, 1 1-2 pounds of sausage meat, and 1-4 pound of salt pork. The ham, pork, and tongue are cut in fillips. The tongue may be either fresh or salted, best fresh, and must have been boiled well.

Spread the chicken flat. Lay on a layer of sausage meat. Then a layer of fillets of ham and pork. Then a layer of sausage meat. Another of fillets, till you can get enough to fill the chicken. You can put in the legs and wings and a few fillets of truffles if you wish. Fold up the chicken so as to cover the meat, &c., and sew up, and leave a little space open so that you can see in. Roll it up in a large towel. Put it in a pot, with the same seasoning as for broth, and cover with cold water. Boil gently three hours.

It will sink at first, and when cooked it will rise above the water. You may put the bones and trimmings of the same chicken in to make broth if you choose. When cooked take it off in the pot and let the pot cool with the chicken in it. Take it out, lay it on its breast, towel and all, with a weight on it, over night. That will flatten it, and next day lay it on a plate, breast up.

65.—P A T E.

A pie usually made with game. In the absence of that we use a pigeon. When cleaned put it in a bakepan. Lay a slice of salt pork on the breast and place it in the oven for an hour or more.

For the paste. We have four ounces of flour, two of butter, a pinch of salt, half a gill of cold water, mixed to a paste. Line the bottom and sides of a flat pan with the paste. The bird is carved as if for the table, and the pieces laid in, and paste covered over the top. Put a little broth or gravy inside, and leave an opening in the top for the steam to escape. Color the top with a yolk of egg and bake. It may be eaten either hot or cold, and will keep a week or ten days, as wanted.

Truffles may be baked in a pate, two ounces to a pound of meat, but in that case it is best to have no bones in the pan, only clear meat.

66.—DUCK WITH TURNIPS.

Clean the duck. Cut off the end of the legs. Run a trussing needle and twine through the body and wings, so as to tie the wings down, and do the same with the legs. Always take out the crop by cutting off the neck and cutting a slit in the back of the neck, so as not to spoil the look of the breast.

Put a piece of butter as large as a walnut in the saucepan. When melted lay in the duck, and keep turning it till browned. Take out the duck and put a teaspoonful of flour in the pan and stir. When the flour is browned, add half a pint of broth and stir, and put the duck back into the pan, a bunch of seasoning, (two stalks of parsley, one of thyme, and a bay leaf,) a whole onion with two cloves, one clove of garlic, and simmer.

Put some fat on the fire in a pan. When hot turn in your turnips cut in moderate sized pieces. When browned put the turnips in the pan where the duck is. Skim off the fat well. When done (an hour and a half or so) take out the duck and untie it; take out the bunch of seasoning.

67.—PIGEON IN CHARTREUSE.

When there are no partridges or prairie hens at hand, use a pigeon. Cut carrot and turnip in small pieces, and boil till done. Take a mould and grease it. Line it with the pieces or squares of carrot and turnip in regular form.

Throw cabbage or cabbage sprouts in water at its first boiling, and when that is cooked, drain in a culander. Fry the cabbage in a little butter. Put a layer of cabbage in the mould.

Bake the pigeon quick, without anything in the pan. Cut up the pigeon and lay on the mould in the cabbage some pieces of the pigeon. Another layer of cabbage. Use only salt and pepper. Pour the juice from the bakepan over the whole. It is more an ornamental dish than a tasteful one. Set the mould in a pan, half-deep in boiling water, and set in the oven.

68.—CHICKEN A LA MARENGO.

After the battle of Marengo, Napoleon wanted a chicken saute, and for want of butter oil was used.

Cut the chicken in a dozen pieces. Put four table-spoons of olive oil in a saucepan on the fire, and fry the chicken in it. When browned take out the pieces and put them in another saucepan without the oil. Put in with the pieces a tablespoon of flour, and stir. Add a gill of wine and a gill of broth. Salt and pepper to taste. Put in two stalks of parsley and two cloves of garlic, tied together, and a bay leaf.

Put the oil back on the fire. Fry small square slices of bread in it till they are brown. Also, one or two eggs, and serve with the bird.

69.—SALMIS

May be made with any wild bird or with a duck. Cooked bird must be used, cold or warm.

Put butter and flour in a pan. When melted, add a little warm water or broth, a bay leaf, and a bunch of parsley and thyme. Put in the bird in reasonable sized pieces.

70.—CIVET.

May be made with rabbits, venison or goose. A tablespoon of butter in a saucepan. Cut your goose in pieces and put it in. It is better to skin the goose and remove the fat. Stir so as to brown the pieces. Put in a little flour and stir. Then warm water, and a gill of claret wine, two onions, a bunch of seasoning made of parsley, thyme, bay leaf and garlic tied together. After a while add two mushrooms.

71.—STUFFED CHICKEN.

Half a pound of sausage meat set on the fire in a saucepan and stir. Then a handful of bread soaked in water, and squeezed out. Two stalks of parsley chopped fine. After stirring a little add one egg, and take it off. Stuff the chicken with the mixture. Any kind of bird may be stuffed in the same way. Sew the bird up, truss it as when you roast, and bake it.

This is served either as an entree or a roast piece.

A chicken may be stuffed with whole roasted chestnuts or with truffles.

72.—JELLY FOR BONED CHICKEN.

Take four calf's feet. Set on the fire with two and a half qts. of cold water. Boil till tender. Strain through a culander. Put the juice on the fire. Beat two whites of eggs and four ounces of liver chopped fine, and put it in the jelly. Put the whole into a jelly bag. The jelly may be spread over a chicken boned, in small pieces or any other way.

VEGETABLES.

73.—ASPARAGUS.

Should be thrown into boiling hot water, salted, and boiled till three-quarters cooked. Longer boiling makes them tasteless. A spoonful of butter and flour melted in a pan, with half a pint of hot water added and stewed, makes a good sauce.

74.—FRIED ASPARAGUS.

Four tablespoonfuls of flour, salt, cold water, stirred together in a bowl to a thick batter. Beat two whites of eggs to a stiff froth, and stir in with the rest.

Throw the tops of asparagus in boiling water, with a little suet, till half done. Then throw them in the batter, hook them out and fry with hot fat.

75.—ASPARAGUS IN PETIT FOIS.

These tops were broken in small pieces like peas, and put in a saucepan. Put in boiling water, with salt, and cook till three-quarters done. Always use the water as soon as it boils, for there is more alkali and gases in it then than afterward.

As soon as done, put them in a culander and drain. A teaspoonful of butter and flour mixed on the fire. Put in a gill of the asparagus. Stir it. Then mix it in the asparagus. Salt and pepper to taste.

76.—POTATOES IN CROQUETTE.

The potatoes were cooked by steaming. Peel and mash through a culander. Put them in a saucepan on the fire, with an egg-sized piece of butter to six potatoes. Salt and pepper. Take off the fire. Mix in three eggs. In two minutes take them out into a dish and cool.

Roll lumps of the mashed potato in flour, then dip

in egg to make the outside sticky, then roll in bread crumbs, and cook in hot fat on the fire.

77.—MASHED POTATOES.

Wash clean with a scrubbing brush. Do not peel before cooking. The potatoes may be steamed, then put in cold water and boiled, mashed through a culander, the yolks of three eggs mixed in, a table-spoonful of granulated sugar added, then the beaten whites of the eggs. Put in tin pans in the oven till ready for use.

78.—POTATOES A LA PARISIENNE.

When you prepare the potatoes scrape them, drop them in cold water, to keep them white. Cut in thin slices. (When cut into fillets or thin slips like a pencil, it makes potatoes Francaise).

Cook the potatoes in hot fat, and take them off when three-quarters done. After a few minutes put them again in the same fat, and in a short time take them off with a skimmer, and pepper, and serve warm.

The object in taking the potatoes out of the fat when they were three-quarters done, was to allow them to swell, and render them better eating. Potatoes swell considerably.

79.—POTATOES A LA LYONNAISE.

Steam the potatoes with the skin on. Peel. (Boil them, if you can do so better).

With eight potatoes, put one, two, or three large onions. Fry the onions sliced, with butter, in a pan. When browned, put in the potatoes in slices.

80.—POTATOES A LA DUCHESSE.

Steam three or four potatoes till well done; peel them, and mash them through a culander, into a bowl; mix in two eggs, and a piece of salt.

Grease a pan with butter. Put in the potatoes with a spoon in separate lumps, flattened out, and put them into an oven.

81.—POTATOES IN SALAD.

Butter, vinegar, salt, pepper and chopped parsley.
Slice hot potatoes, and turn them into a frying pan
in which there is a little butter. When fried take
them off and spread over them the parsley mixture,
and serve.

82.—SPINACH.

Throw them in boiling water, a little salt, and boil
till tender. Chop it up. Add a spoonful of butter
and stir, salt and pepper to taste, a little grated nutmeg, and stir. A table spoonful of flour next, stirred
well in. Then stir in a gill of broth.

83.—SPINACH.

At the first boiling of the water put in a quart or
so of spinach, and a little salt, and boil some. Take
out, and press in a culander, to get out the water.
Then spread on a board and chop a little. Put on
the fire a pan, with a little butter. When melted,
stir in a tablespoonful of flour, and afterward the
spinach. Salt and pepper to taste. A little grated
nutmeg. Some persons add sugar. Cook. Add a
gill of milk. Cream is better.

84.—DANDELION STEWED.

Dandelions thrown into boiling water, and when
cooked, drain in a culander, and chop them up.
Put half a tablespoonful of butter and flour in a
pan on the fire, and stir till browned. Add the
chopped dandelion, a little broth and stir.

85.—TURNIPS AND SUGAR.

Slice the turnip in dice in a saucepan, and throw
in boiling water to blanch them. When three-quarters done, take them out. Put them on the fire with
a teaspoonful of butter, stir, and leave it simmering
till done. Then spread sugar on it, and serve.
Turnips glacis are made the same, only butter is
put on them with the sugar, and they are finished in
the oven.

86.—TURNIPS A LA POULETTE.

Cut the turnips in dice in a saucepan. When boiled tender turn them in a culander. Put a little butter and flour in a saucepan, and stir. Add a gill of milk and stir, then the turnips, and salt and pepper to taste.

87.—LETTUCE STUFFED.

Put lettuce (or cabbage) in boiling water to blanch it. In five minutes take it from the water and drain. Place sausage meat between the leaves. Tie the ball of lettuce up with a string. Put it in a small saucepan, with half an inch of broth, on the fire.

88.—PEAS AU NATUREL.

Take half a peck of peas. Shell them. If old, blanch them in boiling water for a minute. Young peas do not need it. Take out the peas with a culander. Put them in a pot on the fire, with a little salt, two teaspoons of sugar, a head of lettuce. Tie together three stalks of parsley, and a bay leaf, and put in. Also a piece of butter the size of an egg. Stir once in a while.

89.—MACEDOINE.

Cut small pieces of carrot and turnip in water, with salt, &c., and boil gently till tender. Strain off the water through a culander.

Put half a tablespoon of butter and flour in a pan on the fire; add half a gill of broth; turn in the carrot and turnip, and simmer a little.

90.—TO KEEP TOMATOES.

Set them on the fire with a little salt, and reduce one half. Let it cool, and put it in claret bottles. Cork, and tie down the corks. Set the bottles on the fire in cold water, and boil four hours. Take them off, and let them cool in the water. Afterward keep the bottles in a dark place.

91.—CAULIFLOWER.

Throw it in boiling water, with a bit of soft bread, to blanch it. In a few minutes, when done, take it from the fire, and drain through a culander. It can be served as a salad.

Cauliflower may be fried in butter, as asparagus is.

92.—CUCUMBER STUFFED.

Split them in two down the centre, and soak in cold water an hour or more. Then dig out most of the inside of each half. Put the inside in a towel and wring the water out. Chop the inside fine with some sausage meat, salt and pepper to taste. Then fill the outer halves or shells with the mixture. Put them in a pan open part up. A little slip of skin cut off the bottom will make them stand straight and secure. Sprinkle a little salt and pepper and put them in the oven.

93.—BEANS AU JUS.

Soak a pint of white beans in cold water twenty-four hours. Then set them on the fire with a quart of water and a little salt. When cooked turn them in a culander. Then put them on the fire again, with a little broth, chopped parsley, salt, pepper, boil slightly, dish and serve.

94.—GENERAL REMARKS.

Cucumbers sliced for the table should always lay with salt on them fifteen minutes, and then the water be thrown away.

To make the toughest greens tender, soak them in water twenty-four hours before cooking.

To boil carrots, parsnips and turnips, in slices, put either in cold or warm water and boil gently (with salt) till tender.

CAKE, PASTRY, &c.

95.—PUFF PASTE.

Puff paste requires good dry flour, if not **dry** enough dry it in a warm place, not a hot one; have good butter, and if salt it can be worked out in cold water; it is best to roll puff paste on marble, and the cooler the better to keep the butter from leaking out; the rolls may be cooled on ice.

Take half a pound of flour, make a hole in the middle, put in salt, and a gill of water, and mix a thick paste or dough. Roll it out a quarter of an inch thick. Spread a half pound of butter over it. Fold it from each side toward the centre, so it will be folded three folds, then from each end likewise. Set it in a cool place for some minutes. Then roll out and fold again. Repeat this folding and rolling out four times, at intervals. The last time you roll out, you can sprinkle flour if it sticks. This is your puff paste.

Puff paste requires a very hot oven. After putting it in do not open the oven for ten minutes, or it will fall. The oven used by the Professor marked 400 degrees.

96.—MADELINE CAKE.

Half a pound of eggs (four), half a pound of butter, half a pound of sugar, half a pound of flour. Mix the butter, sugar, and yolks of the eggs thoroughly, then add the flour and mix again, then the whites of the eggs beaten to a thick froth. Grate in a little lemon rind. Put it in little dishes, filling each about one-third full, and bake till done.

In these cakes the butter and sugar were thoroughly mixed, and the yolks of the four eggs added one at a time. The flour was afterwards rubbed in, and then the frothed whites of the eggs.

97.—PIE.

Take puff paste for the top. For the bottom crust take a half pound of flour, half a tablespoonful of butter, a little salt, and mix with cold water till thick enough. Roll it very thin. Spread it in your pan or plate. Put in your preserves or fruit, always cooked before-hand. Spread puff paste on the top. Color the top paste with the yolk of an egg, and bake in a quick oven. Do not open the oven for ten minutes.

98.—BOUCHEES DE CREME.

To make Bouchees, after puff paste is rolled out, cut with a cutter little cakes with a hollow in the centre, and place on pans. Color the top with a little yolk of egg mixed with water, and bake in a quick oven.

The Petites Bouchees may be filled either with sweetmeats or fruit, or with patisserie or frangipauni.

99.—FRANGIPANNI.

This can be served as it is, cold, as a dessert, or as an entremet. Put two ounces of flour in a clean saucepan (on the table), and mix in two eggs; grate in a little orange or lemon rind to flavor it, then stir in two ounces of sugar; then one quart of milk; an egg beater is good to mix with. Now set it on the fire, and stir it constantly. This was on seven minutes.

100.—CAKE WITH ALMONDS.

Pound two ounces of sweet blanched almonds with two ounces of fine white sugar. Mix in a bowl two ounces of sugar, and four yolks of eggs. Mix the almond paste into the bowl little by little. The almonds may be blanched or skinned by being dipped a short time in boiling water, when they peel easily. Wash the mixture in your bowl well. The four whites beat to a stiff froth and mix in well with the rest. Mix in four ounces of flour, sifted, and dried in a gentle heat. Put all in a butter-greased mould. Put it in the oven. It need not be very quick.

101.—ANOTHER CAKE.

Four ounces of butter, four ounces of sugar, mixed in a bowl. Mix in four whole eggs broken into the bowl. Then four ounces of flour, essence to flavor; mix well and bake.

If you add two to four ounces of almonds, pounded with a little sugar, you have a third kind of cake.

When your almond cake is done cover the mould with a damp cloth.

102.—PATE A CHOUX.

This is more difficult to make than puff paste. Put three gills of cold water on the fire in a saucepan, and when it boils throw in two ounces of butter, a pinch of salt, and soon after add six ounces of dried flour. Work the flour over the fire. If the fire is too hot remove it a little. Work it till it will not stick to the finger on touching, and is soft as velvet. Let it cool in a large bowl on the table. Grate in lemon or orange rind to taste. Mix. Break in an egg. Mix well. Three more eggs, one at a time, mixing after each.

Grease a bakepan with a little butter. Put the paste in in little round balls, with spoon and finger, balls well apart, and the size of a black walnut; cover the top with yolk of egg and feather. Bake in a quick oven (say 400 degrees).

After you take them from the oven let them cool. Cut a piece off the top, fill up the inside with the cream patissiere, and put on the top again.

103.—CREAM PATISSIERE.

One teaspoonful of flour in a saucepan on the table, with one gill of milk, and mix. Strain through a sieve. Set it on the fire, with a little orange rind to flavor, and keep stirring. Add soon another gill of milk, and boil a few minutes till thick. Stir con-

B

stantly. Have four yolks of eggs in a bowl, and turn in the milk and flour, stirring fast. Put them back into the pan with two ounces of pulverized sugar, put on the fire and stir, and in a minute more turn it out into a bowl, and it is made.

104.—CREME RENVERSE.

One quart of milk, with a little lemon mixed, and three ounces of sugar, in a pan on the fire.

In another small pan (tin mould) two tablespoons of sugar and two of water, and brown on the fire, so that it is not quite burned. Turn the mould in all directions till the browned sugar lines the whole mould, warming it to keep it soft, so you can complete the operation. Cool it.

The pan of milk must be kept stirring till it boils up once. Put in a bowl about five eggs, and turn in the milk little by little, beating with an egg beater at the same time. Turn it into the brown mould with a strainer. Set the mould in a pan of boiling water, and put the pan in the oven.

In this case the pan was kept in the oven twenty-three minutes, then taken out and put away to cool.

105.—GATEAU DE PITHIVIERS.

Take two ounces of blanched almonds and chop them fine. Put them in a bowl with two ounces of sugar, two ounces of butter, and mix. Put in two yolks of eggs and mix. Grate in orange rind, to flavor, or a few drops of essence. Then four macaroons, broken up, and mix again.

Roll out your puff paste to a quarter of an inch in thickness. Place it in a tin plate, spread the mixture over it, and cover the mixture with puff paste. Go around the edges with a pressure, so as to make them stick together. Put in a warm oven, not too quick.

106.—CROQUIGNOLLES.

Put on the board a half pound of flour; add one ounce of butter, lemon rind, two eggs, and a table-

spoon of sugar; mix. Add a third egg; mix well.
Roll out; cut into squares or circles, or rather shapes,
as large as you want them; cut slits across the
squares, nearly from end to end.

Have hot fat on the fire. When it steams it is hot
enough, or when a drop of water hisses. Fry the
croquignolles in it. None of the fat goes into them.
When browned to suit, put in a culander to drain.

107.—MERINGUES.

Beat up the whites of eight eggs in a bowl to a
stiff froth. Add one ounce of white sugar to each
egg (half a pound in all), and mix in little by little
by beating.

Grease a bakepan with a little sweet oil. Then
dust it with flour, and turn it upside down, to get
the loose flour off.

Put the mixture in spots over the pan, an inch or
two apart, with a spoon. If you want them small,
use a teaspoon, if large a larger spoon. Place the
pan in a mild oven (300 degrees or less).

Beat some cream to a froth, and skim the froth
into a bowl. Put gelatine, with a little cold water,
on the fire. Melt it and stir it into the bowl of
cream. One ounce of gelatine answers for a pound
of cream.

When the Meringues are baked and cool, cut out
the bottom, fill with the cream, and put two together,
tops out. Put no flour in the cream.

108.—GENOISES.

Five ounces of butter warmed. Mix into it in a
warm bowl six ounces of sugar. Mix in five ounces
of flour. Then break in and mix six eggs, one at a
time. A teaspoonful of Jamaica rum. Work it
well.

Grease a shallow tin pan with a little butter. Pour
in your paste to the depth of a third of an inch. Set
it in a quick oven, but not too quick. When baked
twenty minutes or more, turn it over into another

pan, and put it back in the oven.　In a few minutes it will be done.　Then let it cool.

The genoise is cut in pieces of any shape or size.

109.—CREME AU CHOCOLATE.

Cream with chocolate, or chocolate custard.　One pint of milk and two ounces of chocolate, boiled a little.　Mix four yolks and two whites of eggs, and mix with the milk.　Set the cups in a pan of hot water, and put the pan in the oven.　When cooked, take out the pan and set it in a cool place.

110.—CREME AU CAFE.

Cream with coffee—a coffee custard.　Beat together two yolks of eggs and two whole eggs in a bowl, with a tablespoonful of sugar.　Add one pint of cold milk and a half gill of very strong liquid coffee.　Mix it all and pass it through a strainer into cups.　Set the cups in a pan of hot water, which comes half way up the sides of the cups, and put the pan in the oven.　When baked take out the cups and cool.

111.—CREME AU CITRON.

Cream with lemon, or lemon custard.　One pint of milk in a saucepan on the fire, with a couple of pieces of lemon rind.　When the milk rises, add two tablespoons of sugar, and stir a little.　After you have made it once, you can tell whether you want more or less of lemon or sugar.　Beat the whites of four eggs and the yolks of two in a bowl, and treat the whole as you did the creme au cafe or coffee custard.

112.—CREME AU THÉ.

Cream with tea, or tea custard.　One pint of milk in a small saucepan.　When it rises take it off, and put in a tablespoon of dry tea (never use green).　Let it stand on the table some minutes to draw.　Take three tablespoonfuls of sugar, four yolks and two whites of eggs, mixed in a bowl, and add them

to the tea, and stir well. Then strain into a mould
or cups, and bake them in the same way as the creme
with coffee, or coffee custard.

113.—JELLY WITH STRAWBERRIES.

Three ounces of gelatine in a tin saucepan, with
four sticks of cinnamon, a little grated nutmeg, and
one quart and half a pint of cold water. Cut into
it the rind of a lemon, and squeeze in the juice.
Add half a pound of sugar.

Four whites of eggs are beaten to a stiff froth,
and also the shells. Turn this into the pan with the
rest. Set it on a brisk fire, and stir with an egg
beater slowly. In ten minutes take it off, and set it
on a slower part of the fire fifteen or twenty minutes.
Strain it through a coarse bag several times till quite
clear.

For strawberry jelly add a little Madeira wine.
Fill the mould one-third full, and set it on ice to
harden a little.

When cool press a layer of strawberries into the
jelly, and pour on more jelly, and set it to cool. If
desirable, a second layer of strawberries may be
added before filling up the mould.

114.—JELLY MACEDOINE.

Prepare your jelly as in the case of strawberries.
After your mould is one-third full, put in a wineglass
of rum and set the mould on ice.

In the rest of the jelly put in two tablespoons of
burnt sugar, and fill the mould another third and
cool. Then add more sugar to the rest of the jelly,
fill up the mould and cool again. By doing this
with fifths instead of thirds, you can make the color
gradual from the top to the bottom, or shaded.

115.—PROFITEROLLES AU CHOCOLATE.

The paste for these is made the same as for the
beignets or for choux, and baked in small cakes.
When done, open one side and fill with chocolate, as
they are hollow. The chocolate is prepared by being

melted with water, and thinned with hot milk to a paste, and a little sugar. The melting of the chocolate requires a teaspoon of water to a couple of ounces, on the fire.

A little more baking smooths the chocolate.

Petits pains au chocolate—This is made by filling the cakes with a mixture of half chocolate and half patissiere cream.

Petits pains a la reine—This is filling the cakes with peach preserve and chopped almonds, mixed.

Eclair au Chocolate—This is made by filling the cakes with frangipanni. A little sweetmeat on the top, covered with chocolate.

Eclair aux Fraises—Fill the cakes with strawberries, either fresh or jellied, with chocolate on the top.

Eclair au Cafe—Fill the cakes with any kind of cream, mixed with a little very strong coffee or essence, and covered with chocolate.

116.—CHARLOTTE RUSSE.

One ounce of gelatine, two tablespoons of water, on the fire to melt. Beat one pint of pure cream in a bowl till it is thick or frothy. Put in two tablespoons of sugar and stir. If your cream is not very thick you may add the melted gelatine. Flour or not, as suits you.

Line the bottom of a tin mould with sponge cake, baked thin and flat for the purpose, and also the sides. Pour in the cream described above, and set it aside, or on ice, till cold. If you desire you may take off the top crust, and substitute for it cream renverse or patissiere, or any other cream.

117.—BEIGNLETS SOUFFLES.

Three gills of cold water on the fire, with two ounces of butter. When it boils stir in six ounces of flour gradually, and stir fast till it does not adhere to the finger, and is soft. Take off and bowl it. Let it cool a little. Stir it some. Stir in four or five eggs gradually.

When your fat in the pan is hot enough drop the paste in in little lumps. As they brown they will turn themselves over in the fat. They will naturally swell five times their size.

118.—RICE CAKE (OR PUDDING).

Take a tin pan and grease it so as to make bread crumbs stick to the inside all over.

Wash four ounces of rice and put it in another vessel with a pint and a half of milk, on the fire. When cooked, add three tablespoons of sugar. Simmer five minutes more. Put the rice in a bowl to cool. Stir in four or five yolks of eggs. Beat the four whites to a stiff froth, and mix it in. Put it in the pan spoken of at first, and put it in the oven. Grease a piece of paper if your oven is too hot, and lay it on top of the cake.

119.—SAUCE FOR THE RICE.

A small tablespoon of butter and one of flour stirred on the fire. Then a tablespoon of sugar and a gill of water, a little piece of lemon rind. Drop in a little white wine and the sauce is done.

120.—SPONGE CAKE.

Ten yolks of eggs in a bowl, with a pound of powdered sugar, and mix well. A few drops of essence, or rind of lemon or orange, or a little nutmeg, to flavor. Mix in half a pound of flour. Afterward mix in the whites of ten eggs beaten to a stiff froth. Bake in a pan or mould.

121.—BISCUIT GLACE A LA ROYALE.

Two tablespoons of powdered sugar, and half the white of an egg worked in a bowl. Add occasionally a drop of lemon juice. It makes the sugar white.

Bake sponge cake in a mould, and when done turn it out and spread the sugar on top, and place it in the oven to glaze the sugar.

122.—BABA.

Mix in a bowl twelve ounces of butter, twelve ounces of flour, nine eggs, four tablespoons of yeast. Mix it in a cool place, to keep the butter cool. Mix it hard with the hand. Add four ounces of currants, four of raisins, four ounces of citron cut in small fillets, lemon or orange rind to flavor, and a glass of whiskey, brandy, wine or other liquor, to taste, a little salt. Set it to rise twelve to twenty hours in the bowl. Bake.

123.—COCOA-NUT CAKE

Is made just like macaroons, using cocoa blanched, instead of almonds.

124.—BRIOCHE.

Twelve ounces of flour in a bowl, with twelve ounces of butter, nine eggs, four tablespoons of yeast, and mix well. The success depends on the working of it. Put in a little salt. Mix it hard with the hand. It must be set aside to rise, from twelve to twenty hours. It is best to make it in the evening. Set it to rise in the bowl.

125.—MACAROONS.

Four ounces of sweet almonds, a little water, a teaspoon of sugar, a few drops of white of egg, pounded in a mortar. When well pounded add six ounces of sugar, one white of egg not beaten, and pound again.

Dip your hands in a bowl of cold water, roll your mixture in little balls, and put them in a pan without any grease. Put it in a slow oven, as they must dry a great deal.

VARIETIES.

126.—COFFEE.

For a quart of water you may take anywhere from an ounce to half a pound, as you please. Two ounces of Rio, two of Mocha, two of Martinique, to a pound of Java, makes a good mixture. To those who can roast it *well* at home, it is best to try the whole berry. Keep your roasted coffee in tin, tightly stopped, and grind it daily. It is impossible to roast coffee properly by steam. Dealers buy coffee at forty-five cents, sell it for forty cents, and make large profits. Coffee loses 1-6th of its weight in roasting. Different kinds of coffee take different lengths of time to roast. But the dealers moisten their coffee while roasting, to keep its weight. It is best to roast coffee without taking the cover off the stove. Wood is best to roast with.

Take five tablespoons of the above coffee mixture to a quart of water. He used in this case the new Old Dominion coffee pot. Put the coffee in the sieve chamber of the pot.

At the first boiling of the water turn enough into the pot just to wet the grounds, and then cover it up again. In a minute pour in your boiling water, and set it aside, and after standing a minute or two to settle, it is clear, and ready for use.

If you boil coffee it dissipates the aroma, and extracts the volatile oil, and spoils the taste.

The best time to take coffee after dinner is twenty or thirty minutes after. It is stimulating, and is said to assist digestion. In the morning it is used with milk. If you find indigestion after breakfast, abandon coffee altogether. Never use tea at breakfast. Rye is bad. Roast wheat instead, pound it in a mortar, do not grind, and then use it as coffee.

127.—T E A.

Pour boiling water into the tea pot to warm it. Empty out the water. Put in the tea and a table-spoon of boiling water. Leave it so one minute, to wet the leaves. Then pour in your hot water. Let it stand three to five minutes, but never longer before using. If it stands longer it becomes too astringent, and the flavor is gone.

Never use tea for breakfast. It is too exciting. Some people think they cannot work without it. That is because they have accustomed themselves to it as a stimulant. By habit we can bring ourselves to use poison enough to kill three persons.

Tea is good in damp climates, to keep off fever and ague, after a meal.

128.—CHOCOLATE.

Grate the chocolate. A tablespoon of water to four ounces of chocolate. Put it on a gentle fire some time. When melted pour on hot milk, and it is ready for use. A half pint of milk to an ounce of chocolate is a good average.

129.—CHOCA.

This is half coffee and half chocolate, with milk, and is said to have been devised by Voltaire.

130.—BAVAROISE.

Take an ounce of chocolate and half a pint of milk for each person. Make it as per directions given for making chocolate. Put in a few drops of cold tea, and some sugar, and beat. Orange essence is a good flavor. It is excellent to eat cold before going to bed.

131.—ICE CREAM.

A pint and a half of milk in a tin saucepan, with two ounces of sugar, and two eggs, and stir with an egg-beater as soon as you get it on the fire. Continue stirring steadily, and take it off as soon as it is going to boil up. Put it in a bowl to cool, and when cool put the whole in a freezer.

Ice around a freezer is better with one-third salt than with less.

To make strawberry cream you squeeze the juice out of strawberries and add it to the milk at first. The riper the strawberries the richer the color. In winter cochineal is used to color. It may be obtained of the leading confectioners.

132.—ROMAN PUNCH.

Infuse an ounce of tea over night in half a pint of cold water.

One pound of sugar and three gills of water must be boiled in a saucepan. When cool put it in a bowl with the rind of two lemons and one of orange, cut in pieces. Also the juice of four lemons and two oranges, and add a little cold water. Beat well, add a little of the tea, and as much rum (one to five gills) as you please. Put it in a freezer and freeze. Some people prefer two or three eggs added, beaten to a froth.

Punch is served at different times during dinner, in different connections.

133.—PLUM PUDDING.

Cut four ounces of beef suet fine, and mix it with four ounces of bread crumbs. Four ounces of raisins and seed them, four of currants, one ounce of citron cut small. Essence or lemon rind to flavor, a little nutmeg grated, two ounces of sugar (some prefer brown).

Beat four eggs with two tablespoons of milk. Mix the whole ingredients above stated into it, and incorporate every thing thoroughly. Put in two tablespoons of rum, a teaspoon of salt.

Dip a clean towel in boiling water, sprinkle flour over it. Put the mixture in. Double up the corners of the towel. Tie it as tight as possible. Boil this size three hours. The longer you boil the lighter it is.

When you serve it, pour brandy or rum over it, and send it to the table burning. Serve it in slices.

A little butter, flour, sugar, and wine, mixed together on the fire, makes a good sauce.

134.—BREAD AND ROLLS.

One half pound of potatoes, steamed with skins on. When cooked mash them with half a pound of flour, half an ounce of salt, half a pint of tepid water, and set it in a warm place for about an hour. Then mix into it half a pint either of baker's or brewer's yeast. Pass the whole through a sieve or strainer, to get out the potato skins.

This leaven takes generally ten or twelve hours to rise. As soon as it begins to fall you strain it to get out the potato skins.

After straining you mix with it two pounds of flour, one ounce of salt, and half a pint of tepid water; keep it in a warm place an hour or so, uncovered, till it cracks on the top. Then you knead with it on a board six pounds of flour, and tepid water enough to make an ordinary dough.

135.—OMELET.

Take five eggs, beat them in a good sized bowl, season them with salt and pepper, and throw in a teaspoonful of chopped parsley. Take a frying-pan, put a piece of butter in it, and when melted pour in the liquid egg, and stir with a table-fork, because they cook rapidly.

136.—OMELET AU RUM.

Four eggs, salt and pepper, beat a little with a fork, a teaspoonful of sugar beat in. Put a little piece of butter in a pan. When the butter melts on the fire, turn the eggs in and stir.

When browned, dished, and sugared afterward, it is an omelet au sucre, or sugar omelet.

To make rum omelet, burn a wine-glass of rum, and stir it in.

137.—EGGS AU FROMAGE.

Put two tablespoons of grated cheese in a saucepan on the table, with a teaspoon of butter, four eggs broken in; set it on the fire, and stir two or three minutes. Dish.

138.—EGGS A LA NEIGE (SNOW).

One quart of milk on the fire in a tin pan. Beat four whites of eggs to a stiff froth. When the milk comes to a boil, stir in two tablespoons of sugar, and then the eggs. They must be turned over, and when well curded, taken out with a spoon.

Take the flour yolks in a bowl. Pour over them as you stir, the milk left from cooking the whites. Set on the fire and stir fast, for a minute or more, and when it begins to thicken put it in a dish, passing it through a strainer or not, as you choose. Then lay the curded whites in the dish and serve cold.

139.—LAIT DE POULE.

Put in a tumbler one or two yolks of eggs and a little sugar. Pour boiling water gradually over it, stirring so as not to cook too fast. It is very light, for a sick person, or for a late luncheon.

140.—CALF'S BRAIN STEWED.

Soak the brain in cold water two hours. (Any other brain will do as well). Take it out and take off the skin and the red veins. Then put it in the saucepan at the same time with the broth and wine. Add a bunch of seasoning, parsley, thyme, and a bay leaf, and salt and pepper to taste.

A good way to cook brain is to fry it in batter.

141.—CALF'S TONGUE.

Scald it in boiling water ten minutes. Take it out and scrape off the skin with a knife. Lard it with pork. Bake or roast, and serve it with either a revigote or a piquante, same as with the gravy.

142.—S A L A D.

This is always sent to the table with the roast
piece or with the chicken. First wash the lettuce,
and be particular to drain it of all the water—for
good salad cannot be made with water. A tablespoonful of oil, and half as much of vinegar; salt
and pepper to taste; stir thoroughly.

Professor Blot incidentally remarked that sorrel,
a sourish vegetable, is the best thing to eat in the
Spring, when prepared similar to lettuce. The dandelion also was an excellent field plant. The latter
was designed for our use. In the order of nature it
was the first palatable vegetable that comes forth in
the Spring season, and man should eat it.

143.—CROQUETTES.

These are a sort of mince meat dumpling. Take
some cold veal, chicken, lobster, or tender cold beef,
chopped fine.

Put a half tablespoon of butter in a saucepan on
the fire. When melted, put in a piece of onion
chopped fine. Fry a little. Add half a tablespoon
of flour. When it browns put in the minced meat.
Stir it steadily and add salt and pepper. Then add
a gill and a half of broth, and set the pan a little
off the fire to simmer.

Chop three stalks of parsley fine, and mix it in on
the fire, stirring all the time. Then break in two
eggs, stirring faster. In two or three minutes take
it from the fire and set it to cool. Thus far has
occupied about ten minutes.

When the meat is cold sift some flour on the board;
take a lump of the mince the size of an egg, or
larger, roll it in the fine flour, dip it in a cup of
beaten egg, drain it and roll it in bread crumbs.
Have a quantity of boiling suet or drippings in a
frying pan, and fry the croquettes in them for a couple of minutes, till brown. Put in a culander, and
let the fat drain off.

144.—LOBSTER SALAD.

Cut the flesh in small pieces. Stir in pepper, salt, mustard, olive oil. Spread the salad over the top, and also mayonnaise sauce. Also the coral of the lobster, and boiled eggs cut in fancy shapes. Put flowers around to ornament.

145.—CHICKEN SALAD.

Put raw chicken flesh in a pan with butter, and brown it. Then half cover it with warm water. Cut half a middling sized onion and carrot in slices, two or three stalks of parsley, two cloves, salt and pepper. Boil gently two hours or more. When cold, cut the flesh in small pieces. Cold chicken or other bird left from the day before will do as well. To make a large dish you can add veal. A very good salad is one-third veal, one-third chicken, and one-third celery, cut up and mixed. Put in olive oil, mustard, &c. Lay it on a dish. Spread mayonnaise sauce over it. Decorate with boiled eggs, sprigs of parsley, beets cut in shapes, slices of lemon, shaped, carrot boiled and sliced in shapes, &c., or a rose or two.

146.—FRITTERS.

Use any kind of fruit or berry, or banana. Cut the banana in slices.

Flour, water and salt mixed to a thick batter. Beat two whites of eggs to a stiff froth, and mix with the batter. A little liquor or wine of any kind will improve it. The slices of fruit are dipped into the butter and cooked in hot fat.

147.—PANADE.

A pint of warm water, a large tablespoonful of butter on the fire. Add sugar to taste and a pint of milk. Beat in a bowl one or two or three yolks of eggs, with a little milk, and turn it into the pot, and it is done.

148.—BURNED SUGAR.

Put a little sugar on the fire, and a little water, and let it burn. Then add water and bottle it. It keeps any length of time.

149.—PAIN PERDU (LOST BREAD).

Take stale bread. Cut it in thin slices, and quarter the slices so as to make them a couple of inches square. Turn boiling milk, well sugared, over it.

A little butter in a frying pan on the fire. Dip the bread in egg, then in crumbs, and fry.

150.—VOL AU VENT ⚑

Is made with puff paste, and baked. One pint of oysters in juice on a saucepan on the fire. Skim off the white scum as it rises. Boil up once.

Mix a tablespoon of butter and one of flour in a saucepan on the table. Add one pint of milk, and set on the fire and stir. Salt and pepper. When it begins to thicken, put in the oysters without their juice, stir a little, and set it a little off the fire to keep warm.

Roll puff paste to half an inch in thickness. Cut in small or large cakes. Lay a strip around the edge, and put another flat cake on the top, and bake in a pan. When baked open the top and fill in with the oyster and milk mixture. To make more room inside two strips of puff paste may have been baked instead of one, in making the cake.

151.—OMELETTE SOUFFLEE.

Take a tin mould or pan. Grease it with butter. Mix in a bowl five yolks of eggs and three ounces of sugar. Beat five whites to a stiff froth, and mix them with the yolks and sugar.

Pour the whole into the pan and set the pan in the pan in the oven. An omelette soufflee must be made just before serving, as it falls very soon.

152.—BREAD PUDDING.

Soak a five-penny loaf in milk for ten minutes.

Squeeze the milk out by hand, put the bread in a bowl, and mix in four yolks of eggs, then four ounces of raisins. Beat the four whites to a stiff paste, and mix it with the rest.

Grease a mould with butter, and fill it two-thirds with bread. Set the mould into boiling water for twelve minutes. Set it in the oven and bake.

153.—MACARONI.

Put half a tablespoonful of butter, and the same of flour, in a pan, and mix on the fire. Then a little more than half a pint of milk, and stir. Add salt. This is the sauce.

The macaroni has been boiled in a pan, with a little butter and salt, drained in a culander, and the sauce is poured over it on a dish.

154.—MACARONI AU GRATIN.

Cover macaroni with cold water, a little suet, a little butter, and boil till tender.

Spread butter on the bottom of the dish. Dust it with grated cheese. Then a layer of macaroni. Then a layer of cheese, and so on, as many layers as you choose, the cheese always on top. Salt and pepper, and pieces of butter on top. Put it in the oven.

155.—PUREE FOR FISH OR MEAT.

Set a pint of peas in cold water on the fire, covered. When cooked mash them through a culander, and put them back on the fire, with a little butter. Chopped parsley may be mixed with it.

It can be poured over salt fish, or any other kind of fish or meat, mackerel, &c.

FRUIT, BERRIES, &c.

156.—CRANBERRIES.

Put a quart of water, half pound of sugar, piece of cinnamon in a tin vessel, boil till it honies. Put in a quart of cranberries, shake up to mix, boil fifteen minutes, shaking occasionally.

Raw cranberries can be kept perfectly fresh for three or four weeks by simply putting them in cold water, changing the water every two or three days.

157.—APPLES WITH BUTTER.

Core the peeled apples with a corer. Place in a tin dish. Fill the core hole with sugar. Put a lump of butter on top of the hole, and a little sugar over that again. A little water to cover the bottom of the dish and put in the oven.

158.—CHARLOTTE OF APPLES.

Put one quart of cored and peeled apples, half table spoon of sugar, half gill of water, piece of cinnamon, in a saucepan. Cook. Then strain it through a culander.

Line a tin mould with bread crumbs, using melted butter to stick them on. Put in the apple. Put bread crumbs on top; and set in the oven.

When well baked reverse the pan or mould on a dish and the apple comes out shaped, ready to serve.

159.—APPLES MERINGUEE.

Apples are peeled, cored, seeded. Put them in a saucepan with a table spoon of water, three table-spoons of sugar, and stick of cinnamon. When the apples are done mash them through a culander, and dish.

Three whites of eggs beaten to stiff froth. Mix in

one tablespoon of sugar spread over the apples.
Set in the oven a short time to glaze,

160.—CROQUE EN BOUCHE (CANDIED FRUIT).

Separate an orange or other fruit into pieces, tie a
thread to each piece, and put them in the oven to dry.
Dip them in a white of egg and roll in sugar lightly.

Take currants, on the stalk, wash them, dry them,
dip them in a mixture of egg and water and then roll
them in sugar. When dry the sugar will stick, and
the currants may be served in that form.

Strawberries may be treated in the same way.
They may be made in forms around a cup, by the use
of eggs to stick them together, sugared, and the cup
being drawn out by reversing it, the form will stand.

You put four ounces of sugar and not quite a gill
of cold water on the fire, and boil till it syrups. Dip
your fruit, currants, oranges, or other articles in,
and hang them up by the string to candy or dry.

GENERAL OBSERVATIONS.

161.—A QUESTION ANSWERED.

A lady sent up a piece of paper with the question,
"Is a cook a chemist?"

The Professor's reply was:

"A cook is a person whose duty it is to keep in
order the animal mechanism. A chemist is called
when that mechanism is out of order."

162.—ON ROASTING.

When you roast beef put it as near as you can to
the fire, till there is a crust all round. Baste first

with a little butter. When that crust is formed, remove it further from the fire by degrees. Baste and turn often. Do the same for mutton.

Veal and lamb must be put further from the fire, as they will burn quick. If it be very young lamb, it may be wrapped in greased paper, set close, and basted over the paper.

In roasting birds, always envelope them in paper. Remove the paper ten or fifteen minutes before taking them from the fire, so as to brown them.

To roast quails, roll them up and tie in grape vine leaves. Put slices of thin pork over the leaves and tie again. Then put the quails in the oven. When done serve as they are.

A fish may be roasted, and served after meat. Pickerel or eels roast well.

163.—A WORD ABOUT FISH.

Fish having white flesh are—cod, cusk, haddock, hake, halibut, pollock and whitefish. Sauces used with white flesh fish, when baked, boiled or broiled, are—anchovy, caper, mayonnaise, bechamel, egg sauce, scup and maitre d'hotel. Fish with black flesh are—bass, bluefish, eels, herrings, mackerel, perch, pickerel, salmon, scup, shad, tautog or blackfish and trout. For these use anchovy, tomato, caper, genevoise, maitre d'hotel, mayonnaise, scup or court bouillon sauce. Flounders and smelts. Smelts are always fried.

Fish when done will flake off easily when you try it with a fork.

164.—GARNISHES.

Puree may be served under any kind of meat or fish. Spread it in the dish and lay the meat on it. If you have gravy from the meat, you may mix it with the puree.

You may also, for garnishing, use truffles, potatoes a la Duchesse, potatoes in croquette, water-cress.

Meat may be served with its own gravy, garnished with salad.

165.—PHYSIOLOGICAL REMARKS.

It is proved by physiologists that it is the contraction of the muscles that produces wrinkles. Good food makes the skin clear, develops good forms, and makes people look younger.

Animals are more careful of the selection of their food. Man looks after the food of his pet horse more than he does after his own.

Food should be prepared according to season. In winter we want more fatty matter. Greens eaten freely in spring purifies the blood and removes the extra bile.

Solid meat is better in summer than soups, ragout, &c. Good roast meat will best supply the waste of substance. The amount we eat is not what benefits us, but the amount we digest. A little is better digested than a great deal. A great deal of food stops digestion.

A man's stomach and his mind cannot work together. A half hour's quiet, or only light conversation after dinner, will do very well. Never eat when angry, or immediately after a long walk. Be gay as possible at dinner.

Eat at regular hours good and well prepared food, enough, but not too much. Eat slowly, and masticate well. Never eat anything that does not taste good. Drink slowly, and only moderately. Always leave table with a little appetite.

There is a great difference between rich food and high seasoned food. Chocolate is not too rich, if you add water. Rich food is not stimulating or exciting; hot or seasoned food is.

Pork and veal, to be healthy, should always be overdone.

Speaking of trichninæ in meat, the Professor said that if the meat is overcooked there was no danger from it. Many people have eaten diseased meat without injury. A whole brigade of the French army, in 1783, — and it was an historical fact, — was fed on diseased meat for four or five months; and at the end of that time the men were apparently as healthy as those of other brigades, who ate wholesome meat. The fact of it was, the diseased meat was over-cooked, and the men did not know the difference.

The Professor could not recommend diseased meat, but the object of referring to the subject was simply to show the importance, sometimes, of over-cooking meat.

166.—QUENCHING THIRST.

As to drinking, when you eat you do not feel the effect of it at once. If you drink when warm you do. Wet your hands if you are warm, and then your forehead. Sip the water with a teaspoon. This would have saved many lives of those who die from colds, inflammations, &c., on account of over drinking, or of cold fluids. The thirst is best quenched so, and with one-third of the water otherwise used. Hot coffee or liquor do not quench thirst. By reaction they increase it.

167.—CLASSES OF FOOD.

There are two classes of food, vegetable and animal, which may be subdivided thus : Milk, esculent grains, vegetables, meat, fish, fruit and eggs. In addition to these we have turtle and frogs. There are only eight ways of preparing food, viz: Baking, boiling, broiling, frying, roasting, saute, simmering, and stewing.

HINTS AND ITEMS.

———

Raw oysters are not proper to use at dinner where soup is used, as they spoil the taste of the soup.

In making up a bill of fare, serve in the following order—soup, fish, beef, mutton, veal; poultry, game, &c.

Every kitchen should have a clock in it. Always write down your bill of fare, and the time to begin each article, and put it near the clock—that is, where you have a number of dishes. Have a good cook book, though you do not follow it. It is good for reference in small matters, such as seasoning.

Professor Blot disapproves of self-raising flour and patent yeasts.

A dinner a la Russe, is carved in the kitchen. A dinner a la Française, looks better, as it is carved on the table. Thiers said when he went to the latter he always dined before leaving home.

Brazing is a process used where they have no ovens. It is done in a pan with a hollow cover, which is set on coals, and coals heaped on the cover.

Richelieu devised the Mayonnaise sauce.

Calf's or sheep's feet may be prepared the same as calf's head a la poulette.

Beef suet should always be melted on a slow fire.

Any strong tasted bird may have its taste changed by a sage leaf or two inside, and one or two in the pan.

In cooking use cast iron pans, galvanized with tin linings. A China lining will crack soon, and the food be spoiled. Copper requires a good deal of work, and often in little crevices generates verdigris. Boiling water and washing soda used with a brush will keep clean the galvanized iron.

To make bread crumbs, dry stale bread in the

oven, break it up, roll it with a pin, and pass it through a coarse sieve.

When you cook salt fish, soak it in warm water an hour, to get the salt out. Boil it in cold water. When half cooked, throw the water away, and renew with warm water.

A very good dish may be made by cutting bread into dice, and frying it in fat.

Never eat lobster at or after supper; it is heavy.

Vegetables and fried fish are always entremets.

An omelette may be made more flakey by being set in the oven as soon as done.

No matter what sauce or gravy you make, always skim the top clean, strain the fat into a jar, and keep it for cooking.

Always make your own pickles, if you would be sure that there is no poison in them. The beautiful green of some is produced by poisonous substances.

The best part of a potato is that nearest the skin.

The centre leaf of a radish should always be left on, and eaten with it, as there is something therein that corrects the radish, and prevents indigestion.

The most difficult part of cooking is mixing and seasoning.

In boiling any kind of green vegetable, always put it in when the water first begins to boil.

It does not accelerate cooking to boil fast.

The harder meat is boiled the poorer it will be. Intense boiling not only closes the pores of the meat, but suffers the real goodness to be lost in evaporation.

In putting any kind of ingredients into a given quantity of base, only one at a time should be mixed, as it is impossible to thoroughly mix a number of substances at one and the same time.

To beat eggs most quickly into a stiff froth, is to have fresh eggs; and when the bowl is exposed to a draft or is put on ice, it will become stiff much quicker.

Always grease dough pans with a feather. It is a

great saving of butter. It requires scarcely any butter for this purpose. It is not only dangerous but costly to use the fingers, especially when butter is high. The best fat to use for cooking purposes is beef suet.

The Professor considers it wicked to use soda, saleratus, or cream of tartar in making bread or cake.

A single bay leaf is an addition to a pot of soup.

Bay leaves come often on boxes of figs, as a surface covering, and also in other ways.

Never eat melon for dessert. It should be eaten before dinner.

When you buy a coffee pot, shorten the coffee holder a little, and have a gauze put on the bottom instead of the bars or perforated tin. It draws better.

French cookery is somewhat Italian in its nature. Catherine de Medicis was an Italian. She brought with her into France her mode of cooking, as well as some of her other customs. The Italians borrowed their customs from the Romans, and they, in turn, from the Greeks. A French cook, as soon as he or she discovers a good dish, adopts it, no matter where it may come from. As an instance of this, in France the cranberry is used, but it is a borrowed dish—perhaps American. Mock turtle and plum pudding are English dishes.

A very good soup may be made by boiling turnips, carrots, &c., in broth, and breaking in pieces of dry toasted bread before serving.

Wooden spoons are best for mixing dough.

In cooking never salt your articles fully. People can always salt to suit themselves, at the table.

Many people are disgusted with highly salted food, while others want salt in everything.

Immediately after a substantial meal a person should take half an hour of perfect rest. Do not read. Light, trivial conversation is advisable—anything that rests body and mind together.

Manual labor does not have so injurious an effect as labor of the brain, after eating.

No kind of drink ought to be taken before eating. Drinking when the stomach is empty causes the evaporation of the gases, irritates the stomach, and is very often followed in the end by indigestion and dyspepsia.

The French custom of taking a cup of black coffee after dinner, has been adopted every where. Coffee is a stimulant; it produces agreeable sensations, and excites the faculties of the mind. It helps digestion, after a substantial dinner. It neutralizes the fermentation of alcohol in the stomach to a great extent. Its undue use deranges the liver. Never drink anything too hot or too cold.

It is known in physiology that alcohol causes the food to ferment in the stomach, and partly paralyzes the nervous system, and consequently stops the stomach in its hidden and wonderful work. When wine is used *during* dinner, it should be with three-fourths water, with few exceptions. The true gastronomer, if he drinks wine, never drinks it pure till he comes to the dessert. White wines are the least hurtful, if pure.

Too free use of any beverage, in a warm day, weakens the stomach. A tablespoonful of cool water at intervals of an hour or two, will enable a person to feel stronger and cooler on the whole. Overloading the stomach with fluids in hot weather, causes lassitude, indigestion, and many other unpleasant feelings. Water taken into the mouth freely and ejected will do a good deal to quench thirst.

Many people think they are not fond of sweet oil as food, but like lard. This is all imagination. Great quantities of lard are shipped to Nice, and one or two other places in the south of France, and after certain preparation the lard is returned as olive oil. Three-quarters of the substance of the olive oil of commerce is lard.

I N D E X.